吃当地食物

How We Organize Ourselves | Non-Fiction Series

Copyright © 2022 by Level Learning, INC. and Washington Yu Ying PCS™
Original and Edited Text Copyright © 2022 by Washington Yu Ying PCS™

All rights reserved. No part of this book in whole or part may be reproduced without written permission from the publisher.

Published by Level Learning, INC.

Content Contributors:
Washington Yu Ying PCS™ - Qianyi (Shirley) Zhang, Pearl Zao He You
Level Learning - Jingyao Qi

Illustrations by: Josh Taira

Leveling classification based on Level Learning standard. For full description, visit www.levellearning.com

ISBN 978-1-64040-116-7
Simplified Chinese Edition

About Level Learning:
Level Learning provides a literacy focused curriculum specifically designed for K-12 Chinese as a Second Language classrooms. Our program offers 20 levels of specific and detailed objectives, leveled texts and passages, mastery-based online assessment, and analytics to enable data-driven instruction. Level Learning reading curriculum for both literature and informational text emphasize grammar and comprehension skills to help teachers develop confident and independent Chinese language readers. The non-fiction series of books are specifically designed to support our informational text course based on multiple national standards. To learn more about our entire offering, visit www.levellearning.com.

About Washington Yu Ying PCS™:
Washington Yu Ying PCS is a Mandarin English dual language immersion International Baccalaureate (IB) World school. Yu Ying's mission is to inspire and prepare young people to create a better world by challenging them to reach their full potential in a nurturing Chinese/English educational environment. Yu Ying's comprehensive IB, dual immersion curriculum equips students with global competencies for success in the real world. As a leader in immersion education, Yu Ying is determined to advance Chinese language programs and global citizenry education by helping other schools create and strengthen their Chinese programs. For more information, email: products@washingtonyuying.org

什么是当地食物呢？就是在你居住地附近出产的蔬菜、水果、粮食等。

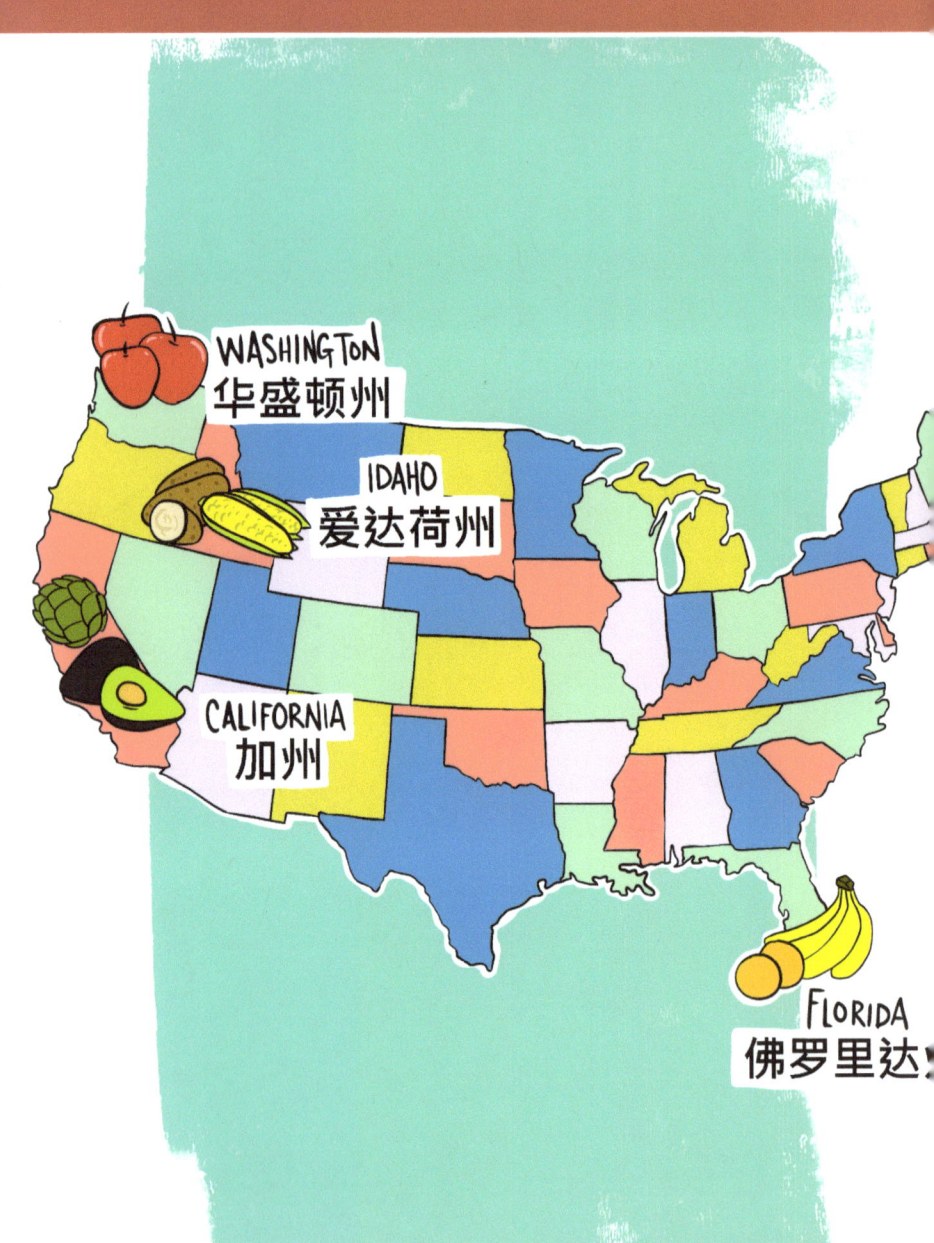

比如说，如果你住在佛罗里达州，当地会出产香蕉和橙子。如果你住在爱达荷州，当地会出产玉米和马铃薯。

吃当地食物有哪些好处呢?

当地的食物更新鲜。比如,刚摘下来的草莓要比从很远的地方运输过来的草莓更新鲜,也更好吃。

运输过程中，汽车和飞机会污染环境。吃当地食物就可以减少污染，保护环境。

吃当地的食物更健康。科学家发现如果食物不新鲜,营养就会流失。所以吃新鲜的当地食物更健康。

吃当地食物可以帮助当地的农民。农民们有了工作，生活就会变得更美好，当地经济也会得到发展。

你觉得吃当地食物还有什么好处呢?

Glossary

	Pinyin	English Definition
当地	dāng dì	local
食物	shí wù	food
居住地	jū zhù dì	place of residence (where you live)
出产	chū chǎn	to produce
蔬菜	shū cài	vegetable
粮食	liáng shi	food
玉米	yù mǐ	corn
马铃薯	mǎ líng shǔ	potato
好处	hǎo chù	advantage
新鲜	xīn xiān	fresh
摘	zhāi	to pick
运输	yùn shū	to transport
草莓	cǎo méi	strawberry
污染	wū rǎn	to pollute
环境	huán jìng	environment

	Pinyin	English Definition
减少	jiǎn shǎo	to reduce
保护	bǎo hù	to protect
健康	jiàn kāng	healthy
科学家	kē xué jiā	scientist
营养	yíng yǎng	nutrition
流失	liú shī	lost
农民	nóng mín	farmer
经济	jīng jì	economy
发展	fā zhǎn	development

www.ingramcontent.com/pod-product-compliance
Lightning Source LLC
Chambersburg PA
CBHW041224070526
44584CB00001B/86